# QUICK & EASY VEGETARIAN

**Photography by Peter Barry**
**Recipes styled by Bridgeen Deery and Wendy Devenish**
**Designed by Richard Hawke and Claire Leighton**
**Edited by Jillian Stewart and Kate Cranshaw**

3561
© 1994 Coombe Books
This edition published in 1994 by Coombe Books
for Parragon Book Service Ltd., Unit 13-17,
Avonbridge Trading Estate, Atlantic Road,
Avonbridge, Bath
All rights reserved.
Printed in Hong Kong
ISBN 1-85813-447-1

# QUICK & EASY VEGETARIAN

PARRAGON

# Contents

# Introduction

People have long dubbed vegetarian cooking slow and laborious, imagining that it involves spending hours in the kitchen preparing elaborate vegetarian specialities. Not so, this book contains a variety of recipes which can be made simply and quickly, with the average cooking time being about twenty minutes.

Although many supermarkets stock quite a number of ready-prepared vegetarian meals, they are often expensive and less tasty than the home-made equivalent. The best supermarket buys for quick and easy cooking are, in fact, fresh vegetables and fruit, pasta, lentils, rice, and canned beans. For speedy preparation, the method, as well as the type of food is important with dishes such as pastas, stir-fries, omelettes and fritters being obvious choices for savoury meals, and fruit, the simple option for desserts. There are also many short-cuts which can be taken by the cook who is short of time. Freezing in particular is a great advantage. When preparing rice, rissoles, pasties, soups, casseroles and bakes, it is a good idea to make a large quantity and freeze some for a later date. When preparing dried beans, instead of soaking overnight, add the beans to three times their volume of boiling water, boil rapidly for two minutes, remove from heat, cover, then leave to stand for one hour before using in a recipe.

Vegetarians tend to have a healthier diet than their meat-eating counterparts, but they must be careful that they eat the correct combinations of plant proteins (rice and beans, beans and nuts, soya and sweetcorn, and pulses and leafy greens with vegetables) to provide the complete protein required by the body for growth and maintenance. For lacto-vegetarians (those who eat diary produce) this is made much simpler as complete protein is provided by milk, eggs and vegetarian cheese.

Preparing quick and easy vegetarian meals does not mean the dishes are any less tasty or impressive, or that they should be reserved for a mid-week meal. Within these pages you will find dishes for all occasions, with traditional vegetarian dishes such as soups and salads, as well as pasta and one pot meals. For entertaining, dishes such as Brazilian Avocados or Fennel and Orange Croustade make impressionable starters; while Mushroom Stroganoff, Pasta Spirals with Walnuts and Stilton, and Sesame Stir-fry make simple but delicious main courses. For a dessert try treating your guests to something delightfully different such as Baked Bananas Sauce a la Poire, or Sautéed Apples with Calvados.

With *Quick and Easy Vegetarian* meals can be exciting and appetising – as well as speedy – allowing you the maximum results with the minimum effort. So next time you have unexpected guests or need a tasty meal in a hurry, this book should provide you with the perfect answer.

# TOMATO AND LEEK SOUP

*This delicious combination of leeks and sweet tomatoes is sure to become a firm favourite.*

*SERVES 4-6*

2 large leeks, washed, trimmed and finely
  sliced
570ml/1 pint fresh tomato juice
Dash Tabasco or soy sauce
¼ tsp celery seasoning
Shake of garlic powder
4 fresh tomatoes, skinned and sliced
Salt and freshly ground black pepper

**1.** Cook the leeks in about 280ml/½ pint of boiling water for 15 minutes or until tender.

**2.** Remove about half the leeks from the cooking liquid and set aside.

**3.** Purée the remaining leeks with the cooking liquid, in a liquidiser or food processor.

**4.** Return the puréed leeks to the rinsed out pan and add another 280ml/½ pint water.

**5.** Stir in the tomato juice, Tabasco or soy sauce, celery seasoning and garlic powder.

**6.** Heat gently to simmering point then add the reserved leeks and tomato slices, and season with salt and pepper. Cook gently for 3-4 minutes and serve hot.

TIME: Preparation takes about 10 minutes, cooking time is about 20 minutes.

FREEZING: This soup will freeze for up to 6 weeks. Freeze in a rigid 1.7-litre/3-pint container.

SERVING IDEA: Serve with crusty French bread and vegetarian Cheddar cheese.

VARIATION: If leeks are not available use large Spanish onions in their place.

# GREEN PEA SOUP

*Pale green and creamy, this delicious soup is made with frozen peas, making it possible to enjoy the taste of summer all year round.*

*SERVES 4*

30g/1oz butter or vegetable margarine
1 shallot, finely chopped
30g/1oz plain flour
280ml/½ pint vegetable stock
420ml/¾ pint milk
460g/1lb frozen peas
¼ tsp dried marjoram
1 tbsp chopped fresh parsley
Salt and freshly ground black pepper
1 small bunch fresh mint
140ml/¼ pint single cream

**1.** Melt the butter or margarine in a saucepan and sauté the shallot until soft.

**2.** Stir in the flour and cook gently for about 1 minute, remove from the heat and gradually add the stock and milk.

**3.** Reserve about 90g/3oz of the peas and add the rest to the pan, along with the marjoram, parsley and seasoning. Return to the heat and cook gently until thickened slightly.

**4.** Pour the soup into a liquidiser or food processor and purée until smooth.

**5.** Using a sharp knife, chop the mint very finely, stir this along with the cream into the puréed soup. Stir in the reserved peas and reheat gently before serving.

TIME: Preparation takes about 10 minutes, cooking takes about 15 minutes.

SERVING IDEA: Serve this soup with crusty rolls and a crumbly vegetarian Cheshire cheese.

COOK'S TIP: Liquidise the soup a little at a time to ensure a smooth texture.

# PARSNIP AND CARROT SOUP

*A delicious and wholesome country soup which makes use of that favourite vegetable, the humble parsnip.*

*SERVES 4*

225g/8oz parsnips, peeled and sliced
225g/8oz carrots, peeled and sliced
280ml/½ pint vegetable stock
570ml/1 pint milk
Salt and freshly ground black pepper
Pinch ground nutmeg
1 small bunch chives, snipped
60ml/4 tbsps single cream

**1.** Cook the parsnips and carrots in the stock until tender – about 15 minutes.

**2.** Place in liquidiser or food processor, and purée until smooth. Return to the rinsed out pan.

**3.** Add the milk and season with salt, pepper and nutmeg, stir in the chives. Reheat gently to simmering point.

**4.** Stir in the cream just before serving.

TIME: Preparation takes about 10 minutes, cooking time is about 20 minutes.

PREPARATION: If a very smooth soup is required, the puréed soup can be strained through a metal sieve before the chives are added.

SERVING IDEA: Serve with crisp French bread and a vegetarian cheese.

FREEZING: This soup will freeze for up to 3 months if frozen before the final addition of the cream. This can be added just before serving.

# CHEDDAR CHEESE SOUP

*An unusual soup which is ideal for using up any left over cheese.*

*SERVES 4*

---

225g/8oz vegetarian Cheddar cheese or a
    mixture of different types of hard
    vegetarian cheeses
45g/1½oz butter or vegetable margarine
1 carrot, peeled and diced
2 sticks celery, chopped
30g/1oz plain flour
420ml/¾ pint vegetable stock
570ml/1 pint milk
1 bay leaf
¼ tsp dried thyme
Chopped parsley, to garnish

**1.** Grate the cheese finely and, if using more than one type, mix together.

**2.** Melt the butter or margarine in a pan and sauté the carrot and celery until just soft.

**3.** Stir in the flour and cook for about 30 seconds. Remove from the heat and gradually add the stock and milk. Add the bay leaf and thyme.

**4.** Return to the heat and cook gently until thickened slightly, stirring constantly.

**5.** Add the cheese a little at a time, stirring until the cheese has melted.

**6.** Remove the bay leaf and serve the soup sprinkled with chopped parsley.

---

TIME: Preparation takes about 10 minutes, cooking time is about 20 minutes.

SERVING IDEA: Serve with caraway or rye bread.

# GAZPACHO

*One of Spain's tastiest exports.*

*SERVES 4*

460g/1lb ripe tomatoes
1 small onion
1 small green pepper
1 clove garlic, crushed
¼ medium cucumber
1 tbsp red wine vinegar
1 tbsp olive oil
1 × 400g/14oz can tomato juice
1-2 tbsps lime juice
Salt and pepper

**1.** Plunge the tomatoes into boiling water, leave for 2 minutes, then remove the skins and seeds.

**2.** Chop the onion and pepper and place in a liquidiser with the tomatoes, garlic, cucumber, vinegar, oil and tomato juice.

**3.** Purée until smooth.

**4.** Add the lime juice and seasoning to taste.

**5.** Pour the soup into a glass dish and chill until required.

TIME: Preparation takes 10 minutes.

SERVING IDEA: Serve garnished with croûtons and finely diced cucumber.

WATCHPOINT: If the soup is too thick, add more tomato juice after Step 3.

VARIATION: Lemon juice may be used in place of the lime juice.

# WATERCRESS AND MUSHROOM PÂTÉ

*A delightful pâté which is perfect garnished with lime or lemon wedges and served with thinly sliced brown bread and butter.*

*SERVES 4*

30g/1oz butter or vegetable margarine
1 medium onion, finely chopped
90g/3oz dark, flat mushrooms, finely chopped
1 bunch watercress, finely chopped
120g/4oz low fat curd cheese
Few drops shoyu sauce (Japanese soy sauce)
Scant ½ tsp caraway seeds
Black pepper

**1.** Melt the butter over a low heat and cook the onion until soft, but not coloured.

**2.** Raise the heat, add the mushrooms and cook quickly for 2 minutes.

**3.** Add the chopped watercress and stir for about 30 seconds until it becomes wilted.

**4.** Place the contents of the pan in a blender together with the cheese and shoyu sauce.

**5.** Blend until smooth.

**6.** Stir in the caraway seeds and pepper to taste.

**7.** Put into individual ramekin dishes or one large serving dish and chill for at least 2 hours until firm.

TIME: Preparation takes 10 minutes, cooking takes 5 minutes.

COOK'S TIP: It may be necessary to stir the contents of the blender several times as the mixture should be fairly thick.

# Brazilian Avocados

*The perfect way to impress your dinner guests right from the first course.*

*SERVES 4*

2 large ripe avocados
A little lemon juice
Salt and pepper
60g/2oz finely chopped Brazil nuts
60g/2oz vegetarian Cheddar cheese, grated
2 tbsps fresh chopped parsley
2 firm ripe tomatoes, skinned and finely
   chopped
Wholemeal breadcrumbs
30g/1oz melted butter or vegetable
   margarine
A little paprika

**1.** Halve the avocados and carefully remove the flesh from the skins. Brush the inside of the skins with a little of the lemon juice.

**2.** Dice the avocado and put into a bowl with a sprinkling of lemon juice and some seasoning.

**3.** Add the nuts, cheese, parsley and tomatoes.

**4.** Mix gently.

**5.** Spoon the filling into the avocado shells, sprinkle with the breadcrumbs and drizzle the butter over the top.

**6.** Dust with the paprika and bake in an oven preheated to 200°C/400°F/Gas Mark 6, for 15 minutes.

TIME: Preparation takes about 10 minutes, cooking takes 15 minutes.

COOK'S TIP: Do not prepare this dish too far in advance as the avocado may discolour.

SERVING IDEA: Serve with a little salad as a starter or with baked potatoes, vegetables and tossed salad for a main course.

# MUSHROOMS AND TOFU IN GARLIC BUTTER

*A quick and delicious starter.*

*SERVES 4*

225g/8oz button mushrooms
2.5cm/1-inch fresh root ginger
225g/8oz smoked tofu
120g/4oz butter or olive oil
4 small cloves garlic, crushed
2 tbsps chopped parsley

**1.** Wipe the mushrooms with a damp cloth.

**2.** Peel and grate the root ginger.

**3.** Cut the smoked tofu into small 1.2cm/½-inch squares.

**4.** Melt the butter in a frying pan.

**5.** Add the crushed garlic and ginger and sauté gently for two minutes.

**6.** Add the mushrooms and cook gently for 4-5 minutes until the mushrooms are softened.

**7.** Finally, add the smoked tofu and heat through.

**8.** Divide between 4 warmed individual dishes, sprinkle with chopped parsley and serve at once.

TIME: Preparation takes 10 minutes, cooking takes 12 minutes.

SERVING IDEA: Serve with Ciabatta bread or crusty wholemeal rolls.

VARIATION: Substitute asparagus tips for the button mushrooms.

# SAVOURY TOMATOES

*An ideal starter for slimmers.*

*SERVES 4*

---

4 large Spanish tomatoes
60g/4 tbsps cottage cheese
1 tsp ground cumin
1 green pepper, diced
Seasoning
60g/2oz pumpkin seeds
1 bunch watercress

---

**1.** Slice off the tops of the tomatoes.

**2.** Cut out the cores and seeds and leave upside down to drain.

**3.** Rub the cottage cheese through a sieve to achieve a smooth consistency, add a little milk if necessary.

**4.** Stir in the cumin, pepper and seasoning.

**5.** Divide the mixture into four and stuff into the tomatoes.

**6.** Dry roast the pumpkin seeds in a frying pan until they are lightly browned. Sprinkle over the tomatoes.

**7.** Chill until required.

**8.** Serve on a bed of watercress.

---

TIME: Preparation takes 10 minutes.

SERVING IDEA: Serve with very thin slices of brown bread and butter.

VARIATION: Use cream cheese in place of the cottage cheese.

# DATE, APPLE AND CELERY STARTER

*A healthy dish with a tasty mix of flavours.*

*SERVES 4*

2 dstsps desiccated coconut
2 crisp eating apples
3-4 sticks celery
90g/3oz dates
2 tbsps natural yogurt
Salt and pepper
Pinch of nutmeg

**1.** Toast the coconut in a dry frying pan over a low heat until it is golden brown, then put to one side.

**2.** Core and dice the apples and chop the celery finely.

**3.** Plunge the dates into boiling water, drain and chop finely.

**4.** Combine the apples, celery and dates in a mixing bowl.

**5.** Add the yogurt, seasoning and nutmeg and mix thoroughly so that the salad is coated completely.

**6.** Transfer to a serving bowl and garnish with the toasted coconut.

**7.** Serve at once.

TIME: Preparation takes 10 minutes, cooking takes 2-3 minutes.

SERVING IDEA: Serve individual portions on a bed of watercress.

COOK'S TIP: Red skinned apples add colour to this salad.

# PAMPLEMOUSSE

*A light and easy starter which is simple to prepare.*

*SERVES 6*

3 large grapefruit
3 red skinned apples
4 sticks celery
24 grapes (black or green)
60ml/4 tbsps double cream

**1.** Halve the grapefruit crossways and cut around the inside of the skin to loosen the flesh.

**2.** Make deep cuts between the segments close to the membranes and remove the segments making sure you do not pierce the skins.

**3.** Put into a large bowl with any of the juice.

**4.** Cut away any remaining membranes from the shells with a pair of kitchen scissors, put the grapefruit shells into a plastic bag and store in the refrigerator.

**5.** Remove the cores from the apples and dice but do not peel.

**6.** Chop the celery finely.

**7.** Halve the grapes and remove any pips.

**8.** Add the apples, celery and grapes to the grapefruit and stir in the double cream.

**9.** Refrigerate until required.

**10.** Just before serving, stir well and pile the mixture into the grapefruit skins.

**11.** Serve at once.

TIME: Preparation takes 10 minutes.

COOK'S TIP: A special grapefruit knife, which has a curved blade, is ideal for loosening the flesh of the grapefruit.

# GARLIC MUSHROOMS

*An established favourite starter, this can also be served as a light snack.*

*SERVES 4*

60g/2oz butter or olive oil
2 cloves garlic, crushed
¼ tsp chopped fresh thyme
¼ tsp chopped fresh parsley
¼ tsp chopped fresh sage
3 tbsps white wine
Salt and freshly ground black pepper
680g/1½lbs mushrooms, cleaned and
 quartered
8 slices of French bread
2 tbsps snipped chives
Fresh herb sprigs, to garnish

**1.** Heat the butter or oil in a frying pan and sauté the garlic until soft.

**2.** Stir in the herbs, wine, seasoning and mushrooms and cook over a low heat for 10 minutes or until the mushrooms are cooked, but not too soft.

**3.** Warm the bread in a low oven, if wished and serve the mushrooms piled onto the bread.

**4.** Sprinkle with chopped chives and garnish with sprigs of fresh herbs.

TIME: Preparation takes about 15 minutes, cooking takes about 15 minutes.

PREPARATION: This recipe can be prepared well in advance and reheated just before serving.

SERVING IDEA: Serve with sliced tomatoes.

VARIATION: Wild mushrooms are often available in good supermarkets; they make a delicious full flavoured variation to this recipe.

# WARM SALAD WITH AVOCADO, GRAPES, BLUE CHEESE AND WALNUTS

*This colourful salad is ideal as a sophisticated salad for a gourmet meal.*

*SERVES 4*

Mixed salad leaves, eg frisee, chicory, radicchio, lamb's lettuce, watercress or iceberg lettuce
2 ripe avocados
Lemon juice
175g/6oz black grapes
15g/4 tbsps chopped fresh mixed herbs
120g/4oz walnut pieces
120g/4oz vegetarian blue cheese, diced or crumbled
3 tbsps walnut oil and grapeseed oil, mixed
2 tbsps lemon vinegar
Pinch sugar

**1.** Tear the larger salad leaves into small pieces and place in a large bowl. If using lamb's lettuce separate the leaves and leave whole. Remove any tough stalks from the watercress. Add to the bowl.

**2.** Halve and peel the avocados then cut crosswise into neat slices. Coat with a little lemon juice and add to the salad leaves.

**3.** Cut the grapes in half and remove the pips. Add the grapes to the salad along with the chopped herbs, walnuts and cheese.

**4.** Put the oils, vinegar and sugar into a screw top jar and shake vigorously until the dressing is well blended.

**5.** Pour the dressing into a large frying pan and heat until bubbling. Remove from the heat and quickly add the prepared salad, tossing well and taking care not to break up the avocado pieces.

**6.** Arrange on individual serving plates and serve immediately.

TIME: Preparation takes about 15 minutes, cooking time is about 2 minutes.

PREPARATION: It is important to tear the salad leaves by hand as the edges will discolour if they are cut with a knife.

VARIATION: Substitute the cheese with 175g/6oz of wild mushrooms that have been sautéed with 2 tbsps of white wine, drained, then chilled.

# MIXED BEAN SALAD

*This nutritious salad is made from a medley of beans, which can be varied according to preference.*

*SERVES 4-6*

175g/6oz cooked red kidney beans
175g/6oz cooked black-eyed beans
175g/6oz cooked butter beans
120g/4oz cooked broad beans, shelled
225g/8oz cooked green beans, sliced
175g/6oz cooked chickpeas
2 tbsps brown sugar
120ml/4 fl oz white wine vinegar
½ tsp salt
¼ tsp black pepper
120ml/4 fl oz olive oil
½ tsp mustard powder
½ tsp dried basil
1 large Spanish or red onion, thinly sliced
   into rings
2 tbsps chopped fresh parsley

**1.** In a large bowl mix all the beans and the chick peas together thoroughly.

**2.** Put the sugar and vinegar into a small bowl, together with the salt and pepper. Stir in the oil, mustard and basil.

**3.** Whisk the vinegar mixture vigorously with a fork, until it becomes thick.

**4.** Pour the dressing over the beans and mix in thoroughly to coat the beans evenly.

**5.** Refrigerate until ready to serve.

**6.** Before serving, mix the onion rings and parsley into the bean salad, reserving a few onion rings for decoration.

TIME: Preparation will take about 15 minutes.

COOK'S TIP: If you cook the dried beans yourself, soak them in separate bowls overnight, and then boil them rapidly in separate pans for at least 30 minutes, before simmering until they are completely tender. Rinse in cold water and drain well.

VARIATION: Stir 120g/4oz of tiny cauliflower florets into the bean salad.

# FENNEL AND ORANGE CROUSTADE

*A delicious mixture which is simple to prepare.*

*SERVES 4*

4 × 2.5cm/1-inch thick slices wholemeal
   bread
Oil for deep frying
2 bulbs fennel (reserve any fronds)
4 oranges
1 tbsp olive oil
Pinch salt
Chopped fresh mint for garnishing

**1.** Trim the crusts off the bread and cut
each into a 7.5cm/3-inch square.

**2.** Hollow out the middles, leaving evenly
shaped cases.

**3.** Heat the oil and deep-fry the bread until
golden brown.

**4.** Drain the bread well on absorbent
kitchen paper. Leave to cool.

**5.** Trim the fennel bulbs and slice thinly.
Place in a mixing bowl.

**6.** Remove all the peel and pith from the
oranges and cut into segments – do this
over the mixing bowl to catch the juice.

**7.** Mix the orange segments with the
fennel.

**8.** Add the olive oil and salt and mix
together thoroughly.

**9.** Just before serving, divide the fennel and
orange mixture evenly between the bread
cases and garnish with fresh mint and
fennel fronds.

TIME: Preparation takes 15 minutes, cooking takes 5 minutes.

VARIATION: Serve the salad on individual plates sprinkled with croûtons.

COOK'S TIP: The salad can be made in advance and refrigerated until
required but do not fill the cases until just before serving.

# COURGETTE SALAD

*Raw vegetables are full of vitamins, and courgettes in particular have a delicious taste and texture.*

*SERVES 4*

225g/8oz macaroni
4 tomatoes
4-5 courgettes, thinly sliced
8 stuffed green olives, sliced
90ml/6 tbsps French dressing

**1.** Put the macaroni into a large saucepan and cover with boiling water. Add a little salt and simmer for 10 minutes, or until 'al dente'. Rinse in cold water and drain well.

**2.** Cut a small cross in the tops of each tomato and plunge into boiling water for 30 seconds.

**3.** Carefully remove the skins from the blanched tomatoes, using a sharp knife. Chop the tomatoes coarsely.

**4.** Mix all the ingredients in a large bowl and chill in the refrigerator for 30 minutes before serving.

TIME: Preparation takes 15 minutes, cooking takes about 10 minutes.

VARIATION: Use any other pasta shape of your choice.

PREPARATION: If you prefer, the courgettes can be blanched in boiling water for 1 minute, then drained and cooled before mixing with the salad ingredients.

# SALADE PAYSANNE

*This homely salad can be made with any selection of fresh vegetables you have to hand. So whether it's winter or summer, there's no excuse for not serving a delicious fresh salad.*

*SERVES 6*

4 spring onions
½ cucumber
3 carrots
6 large tomatoes
10 button mushrooms
3 sticks celery
1 green pepper, chopped
15-20 tiny cauliflower florets
15-20 radishes, quartered
1 tbsp chopped watercress, or mustard and
    cress
2 sprigs fresh coriander leaves, or parsley,
    chopped
8 lettuce leaves for garnish

**Dressing**

½ tsp salt
½ tsp freshly ground black pepper
2 tbsps cider vinegar
1 tbsp lemon juice
60ml/4 tbsps olive or vegetable oil
Pinch mustard powder
Sugar to taste

**1.** Trim the spring onions and cut them diagonally into thin slices.

**2.** Peel the cucumber and quarter it lengthways. Use a teaspoon to remove the soft, seedy centre, discard this, and dice the remaining flesh.

**3.** Peel the carrots and slice them thinly, cutting the carrots diagonally with a sharp knife.

**4.** Cut a small cross into the skin of each tomato, and plunge into boiling water for 30 seconds. Remove the tomatoes and carefully peel off the blanched skins. Quarter the tomatoes and cut away the tough cores.

**5.** Thinly slice the mushrooms and celery.

**6.** For the dressing mix together all the ingredients. Whisk thoroughly using a fork, or ballon whisk, until the mixture becomes thick and cloudy.

**7.** Arrange the lettuce leaves on a serving dish, and pile the prepared vegetables on top.

**8.** Just before serving, spoon a little of the dressing over the salad and serve the remainder separately in a small jug.

TIME: Preparation takes about 20 minutes.

VARIATION: Use any combination of your own favourite vegetables in this recipe.

SERVING IDEA: Serve with vegetarian cheese for a light lunch.

# WHEATBERRY SALAD

*This makes a substantial salad dish which provides an almost perfect protein balance.*

*SERVES 4*

225g/8oz wheatberries, cooked
120g/4oz kidney beans, cooked
3 medium tomatoes, skinned and diced
4 spring onions, chopped
2 sticks celery, chopped
1 tbsp pumpkin seeds

**Dressing**
60ml/4 tbsps olive or sunflower oil
2 tbsps red wine vinegar
1 clove garlic, crushed
1 tsp grated fresh root ginger
1 tsp paprika
1 tbsp shoyu (Japanese soy sauce)
Fresh or dried oregano, to taste
Ground black pepper

**1.** Mix the salad ingredients together, reserving a few spring onion slices and pumpkin seeds for garnishing.

**2.** Shake the dressing ingredients together in a screw-topped jar.

**3.** Pour over the salad and mix gently.

TIME: Preparation takes 20 minutes.

SERVING IDEA: Serve with a lettuce salad. Wheatberries also mix well with grated carrot and an orange dressing.

COOK'S TIP: This salad keeps well so it can be made in advance and kept in the refrigerator until required.

# AVOCADO AND TOMATO SALAD

*This simple salad is very attractive with its bright contrasting colours, and the fresh basil and the dressing bring out the flavours of the avocados and tomatoes.*

*SERVES 4*

2 ripe avocados
Lemon juice
4 medium tomatoes, sliced or quartered
Fresh basil for garnish

**Dressing**
2 tbsps lemon juice
1 tbsp olive oil
Salt
Freshly ground black pepper

**1.** Halve the avocados lengthways, remove the stone and peel.

**2.** Slice carefully and toss in a little lemon juice.

**3.** Arrange the sliced avocado neatly in circles on 4 serving plates and intersperse with the tomatoes.

**4.** Combine the dressing ingredients in a screw topped jar. Shake well and drizzle over the salad.

**5.** Tear the basil into pieces and use to garnish the salad.

TIME: Peparation takes about 10 minutes.

WATCHPOINT: Do not prepare the avocados too far in advance or they will discolour.

# GREEK SALAD

*A great favourite which has the added advantage of being easy to prepare.*

*SERVES 4*

2 tomatoes
½ green pepper
¼ cucumber
2 sticks celery, finely sliced
1 tsp fresh basil, finely chopped
Few crisp leaves of lettuce
120g/4oz Feta cheese, diced
16 black olives

**Dressing**
60ml/4 tbsps olive oil
2 tbsps lemon juice
1 clove garlic, crushed
Large pinch oregano
Salt and pepper

**1.** Cut each tomato into eight pieces and put into a large mixing bowl.

**2.** Roughly chop the pepper and cucumber, and add to the tomato together with the celery and chopped basil.

**3.** Mix the dressing ingredients together and pour over the vegetables, tossing well to coat.

**4.** Arrange a few leaves of lettuce in the bottom of a serving bowl, and pile the salad on the top, followed by the cheese cubes.

**5.** Garnish with the olives and serve.

TIME: Preparation takes 15 minutes.

SERVING IDEA: Serve with pitta bread.

VARIATION: Add a few croutons just before serving.

# LOLLO ROSSO SALAD

*A colourful variation of a Greek Salad.*

*SERVES 4*

½ Lollo Rosso lettuce
3 medium tomatoes, diced
1 red pepper, chopped
1 green pepper, chopped
3 sticks celery, diced
⅓ cucumber, diced
175g/6oz vegetarian Cheshire cheese
16 black olives

**Dressing**
1 tbsp tarragon vinegar
3 tbsps olive oil

**1.** Wash the lettuce and dry it well. Tear into pieces with your fingers and put it into a large bowl.

**2.** Add the tomatoes, peppers, celery, cucumber and cheese.

**3.** Mix together the dressing ingredients, pour over the salad and mix gently.

**4.** Divide the salad between 4 individual dishes and place 4 olives on the top of each one.

TIME: Preparation takes about 10 minutes.

SERVING IDEA: Serve for lunch with crusty rolls or French bread.

VARIATION: If you do not like olives, substitute halved, de-seeded black grapes.

COOK'S TIP: To keep celery crisp, wash well and place the sticks in a jug of cold water in the refrigerator.

# SPINACH SALAD

*Serve with a simple main course.*

*SERVES 4-6*

460g/1lb spinach
1 medium red cabbage
1 medium onion
120g/4oz apricots
90ml/6 tbsps French dressing
60g/2oz toasted sunflower seeds

**1.** Wash the spinach and drain well.

**2.** Remove the outer leaves and core of the cabbage, and slice finely.

**3.** Slice the onion finely and cut the apricots into slivers.

**4.** Tear the spinach leaves into bite-sized pieces and put into a serving dish.

**5.** Add the sliced cabbage, onion and apricots.

**6.** Pour over the dressing and mix together thoroughly.

**7.** Sprinkle with the sunflower seeds and serve immediately.

TIME: Preparation takes 15 minutes.

WATCHPOINT: Spinach leaves bruise easily so take care when washing and tearing the leaves.

COOK'S TIP: If using dried apricots, soak beforehand in a little fruit juice.

# SUNSET SALAD

*Serve this colourful salad with cold nut roasts, raised pies or quiche.*

*SERVES 4-6*

3 dessert apples
340g/¾lb celery
4 medium mushrooms
90g/3oz walnuts
Lettuce leaves
90g/3oz alfalfa sprouts
90g/3oz black grapes

**Dressing**
120ml/4 fl oz mayonnaise
60ml/2 fl oz natural yogurt
Seasoning

**1.** Cut the unpeeled apples into quarters and remove the cores. Dice roughly.

**2.** Dice the celery and slice the mushrooms.

**3.** Chop the walnuts into quarters.

**4.** Mix together the dressing ingredients.

**5.** Put the apples, celery, mushrooms and walnuts into a bowl and fold in the dressing.

**6.** Line a serving dish with well washed lettuce and spread the sprouts around the outer edge.

**7.** Pile the salad in the centre and garnish with the grapes.

TIME: Preparation takes 15 minutes.

COOK'S TIP: Use red skinned apples and lettuce tinged with red, such as Lollo Rosso, to give colour to your salad.

# BROCCOLI AND CAULIFLOWER SALAD

*Serve this simple salad with crackers*

*SERVES 4*

1 red pepper
275g/10oz broccoli
275g/10oz cauliflower
1 tbsp flaked almonds, toasted

**Dressing**
60ml/4 tbsps Greek yogurt
2 tbsps lemon juice
2 tbsps olive oil
Salt and pepper
Pinch of nutmeg

**1.** De-seed the pepper and cut into matchstick pieces.

**2.** Wash and trim the broccoli and cauliflower and break into small florets.

**3.** Place the pepper, broccoli and cauliflower in a mixing bowl.

**4.** Combine the yogurt, lemon juice, olive oil, seasoning and nutmeg in a screw top jar and shake well.

**5.** Spoon the dressing over the salad and mix together well.

**6.** Divide the mixture between 4 individual serving plates and garnish with the almond flakes.

TIME: Preparation takes 10 minutes.

VARIATION: Omit the nutmeg from the dressing and add a few freshly chopped herbs.

COOK'S TIP: Only add the almonds at serving time.

# CREAM SLAW

*The creamy dressing complements the crisp vegetables very well in this salad.*

*SERVES 6-8*

1 medium cabbage
1 large onion
1 green pepper
2 medium carrots
1 dessert apple
2 tsps caraway seeds

**Dressing**
90ml/6 tbsps double cream
3 tbsps natural yogurt
2 tsps French mustard
1 tbsp lemon juice
Seasoning

**1.** Slice the cabbage very finely, removing the outer leaves and core.

**2.** Finely slice the onion and chop the green pepper.

**3.** Grate the carrots and the apple.

**4.** Place all the vegetables with the caraway seeds into a large serving dish and mix together well.

**5.** In a separate bowl whisk together all the ingredients for the dressing.

**6.** Pour the dressing over the vegetables and mix well until all the ingredients are well coated.

**7.** Refrigerate until required.

TIME: Preparation time 15 minutes.

SERVING IDEA: Serve as part of a buffet or with jacket potatoes for a tasty supper dish.

COOK'S TIP: The Slaw will keep for 24 hours if covered and refrigerated, stir well before serving.

# CAULIFLOWER AND FLAGEOLET BEAN SALAD WITH GREEN HERB DRESSING

*Use any herbs for the dressing, but a particularly good mixture is parsley, mint and chives.*

*SERVES 4*

1 small cauliflower broken into small florets
225g/8oz flageolet beans, cooked
120g/4oz mushrooms, sliced
Salt

**Dressing**
30g/1oz finely chopped, mixed fresh herbs
1 clove garlic, crushed
60ml/2 fl oz olive oil
90ml/3 fl oz natural yogurt
1 tbsp lemon juice
Salt and pepper

**1.** Steam the cauliflower for 3 minutes, remove from the pan and leave to cool.

**2.** Blend together all the ingredients for the dressing.

**3.** Mix the beans and mushrooms with the cauliflower and seasoning.

**4.** Toss in the dressing.

TIME: Preparation takes about 15 minutes.

VARIATION: Butter or haricot beans may be used instead of the flageolet beans.

SERVING IDEA: Serve as a side salad, a starter or a light lunch for two people.

# RED HOT SLAW

*This hot and spicy variation of coleslaw makes a delicious and less usual salad that is ideal with highly flavoured dishes.*

*SERVES 4*

460g/1lb red cabbage, cored and shredded

2 red onions, sliced

1 small white daikon (mooli) radish, peeled and grated

60ml/4 tbsps mayonnaise

60ml/4 tbsps natural yogurt

2 tsps grated horseradish

½ tsp aniseed

½ tsp chilli powder

**1.** Combine the cabbage, onions and daikon radish in a large bowl and toss until well combined.

**2.** In a small bowl mix together the mayonnaise, yogurt, horseradish, aniseed and chilli powder.

**3.** Pour the mayonnaise dressing over the cabbage mixture and toss until well coated. Chill until ready to serve.

**4.** Alternatively, serve the cabbage with a little of the dressing drizzled over the top and the remaining dressing served separately.

TIME: Preparation takes about 10 minutes.

COOK'S TIP: Daikon (Mooli) radishes are long white Asian radishes and can be found at delicatessens or ethnic food shops.

# KENSINGTON SALAD

*Decorate the top of this salad with a line of sliced strawberries or kiwi fruit.*

*SERVES 4-6*

3 large mushrooms, thinly sliced
1 medium eating apple, cut into chunks and
    coated with lemon juice
2 sticks celery, cut into matchsticks
30g/1oz walnut pieces
1 bunch watercress

**Dressing**
1 tbsp mayonnaise
1 tbsp thick natural yogurt
½ tsp herb mustard
A little lemon juice
Salt and pepper

**1.** Place the mushrooms, apple, celery and walnuts into a bowl.

**2.** Combine all the ingredients for the dressing and mix gently with the vegetables.

**3.** Arrange the watercress on a flat dish or platter and mound the salad mixture on the top.

TIME: Preparation takes about 10 minutes.

VARIATION: A medium bulb of fennel, finely sliced, could be used in place of the celery.

# NUT AND HERB BULGAR

*Bulgar wheat cooks in a similar way to rice and can be used as an alternative to many rice dishes.*

*SERVES 4*

1 tbsp walnut oil
1 tbsp vegetable oil
1 red pepper, cut into short sticks
1 onion, chopped
30g/1oz pine nuts
120g/4oz cucumber, diced
1 tbsp chopped fresh coriander
1 tbsp chopped fresh mint
2 tbsps chopped fresh parsley
225g/8oz bulgar wheat
420ml/¾ pint vegetable stock
Mint sprigs, to garnish

**1.** Heat the oils in a large saucepan and sauté the pepper, onion and pine nuts for 5 minutes.

**2.** Add the cucumber, herbs and bulgar wheat, then pour in the stock.

**3.** Bring gently to the boil, stir, cover and simmer gently for 10-15 minutes or until the stock has been absorbed. Stir occasionally.

**4.** Serve hot or cold garnished with sprigs of mint.

TIME: Preparation takes about 10 minutes, cooking takes about 20 minutes.

VARIATION: Use brown rice instead of bulgar wheat in this recipe and double stock and cooking time.

SERVING IDEA: Serve with a mixed salad.

# Spaghetti with Pine nuts

*This crunchy flavoursome combination, makes good use of convenience ingredients.*

*SERVES 4*

340g/12oz spaghetti
Salt
90ml/3 fl oz olive oil
1 large onion, sliced
1 clove garlic, crushed
120g/4oz pine nuts
1 × 400g/14oz can artichoke hearts, drained
2 tbsps chopped fresh parsley
60g/2oz vegetarian Cheddar cheese, grated

**1.** Cook the spaghetti in plenty of lightly salted boiling water for 10 minutes until 'al dente', or as directed on the packet.

**2.** Just before the spaghetti is cooked, heat the oil in a frying pan and sauté the onion and garlic until beginning to brown.

**3.** Add the pine nuts and cook for 1 minute, then add the artichoke hearts and parsley. Heat gently for a few minutes.

**4.** When the spaghetti is cooked drain well and add to the pan, tossing until the spaghetti is well coated in the oil.

**5.** Stir in the grated cheese reserving a little to sprinkle on top.

**6.** Transfer to a serving dish and sprinkle with the remaining cheese. Serve immediately.

TIME: Preparation takes about 5 minutes, cooking takes about 15 minutes.

COOK'S TIP: If fresh pasta is used, start cooking the onion and garlic immediately as the cooking time is much shorter.

# VEGETABLE PILAU

*Lightly spiced and fragrant, this traditional Indian rice dish will serve 4 as a
lunch or supper on its own or 6 as part of a larger Indian meal.*

*SERVES 4-6*

60g/2oz butter or vegetable oil
1 onion, finely sliced
225g/8oz long grain rice
1 small piece cinnamon stick
1 bay leaf
Seeds of 4 cardamom pods, crushed
4 cloves
½ tsp ground coriander
¼ tsp ground turmeric
¼ tsp garam masala
Salt and freshly ground black pepper
570ml/1 pint vegetable stock or water
½ aubergine, cut into dice
60g/2oz frozen cauliflower florets
120g/4oz mixed vegetables, diced

**1.** Melt the butter or heat the oil in a large saucepan and sauté the onion until beginning to soften.

**2.** Stir in the rice, spices and seasoning, and sauté for 2 minutes, stirring constantly.

**3.** Add the stock or water and stir well, bring gently to the boil and cook for about 10 minutes.

**4.** Add the remaining ingredients and cook for a further 5-7 minutes or until the rice and vegetables are tender and most of the liquid has been absorbed.

**5.** Leave covered for 5 minutes until the remaining liquid has been absorbed, then stir to separate the grains and serve.

TIME: Preparation takes about 10 minutes, cooking takes about 20 minutes.

COOK'S TIP: Sprinkle with chopped coriander to enhance the taste and give a superb fragrance to this dish.

FREEZING: This recipe will freeze well for up to 2 months.

SERVING IDEA: Serve with a cucumber raita or chutney.

# MUSHROOM STROGANOFF

*A great favourite which is much appreciated by all age groups.*

*SERVES 4-6*

2 medium onions, sliced
5 sticks celery, chopped
60g/2oz butter or margarine
460g/1lb tiny button mushrooms
½ tsp mixed herbs
½ tsp basil
1 large heaped tbsp unbleached flour
280ml/½ pint stock
Salt and pepper
65ml/2½ fl oz soured cream or yogurt
Chopped parsley

**1.** Put the onions and celery into a large pan together with the butter or margarine and sauté over a low heat until the onions are transparent.

**2.** Add the mushrooms and cook for 2-3 minutes until the juices run.

**3.** Add the mixed herbs and basil.

**4.** Stir in the flour and cook for 1 minute.

**5.** Gradually stir in the stock, season and allow to cook gently for 8-10 minutes.

**6.** Remove from the heat, stir in the soured cream and adjust the seasoning if necessary.

**7.** Heat very gently to serving temperature, but do not allow to boil.

**8.** Garnish with the chopped parsley and serve at once.

TIME: Preparation takes 10 minutes, cooking takes 20 minutes.

SERVING IDEA: Serve on a bed of Walnut Rice – cook enough rice to serve 4-6 people and carefully fold in seasoning, a little butter, 1 crushed clove of garlic and 50g/2oz finely chopped walnuts.

COOK'S TIP: If tiny button mushrooms are not available use the larger variety and slice thickly.

# POLYGARDOO

*An adaptable dish which can be served as a snack, side dish or main meal.*

*SERVES 4*

1 onion, finely chopped
1 clove garlic, crushed
1 tsp bouillon powder dissolved in a little
    boiling water
120g/4oz mushrooms, wiped and sliced
1 small green pepper, chopped
1 × 400g/14oz can tomatoes, drained
1 pinch of any herb – oregano, sage, thyme
    or mixed herbs
2 × 400g/14oz can cannellini beans
Salt and pepper
1 tbsp lemon juice
2 tbsps yogurt

**1.** Cook the onion and garlic with the bouillon powder and water until softened a little.

**2.** Add the mushrooms and chopped pepper and continue cooking for 3-4 minutes.

**3.** Add the tomatoes, herbs, beans and seasoning.

**4.** Mix well and simmer gently for 5 minutes.

**5.** Remove from the heat and stir in the lemon juice and yogurt.

TIME: Prepration takes 10 minutes, cooking takes 15 minutes.

SERVING IDEA: Serve with pitta bread, rice or pasta for a main meal.

VARIATION: Any type of cooked beans may be used in this dish.

# LESCO

*A popular recipe from Hungary.*

*SERVES 4-6*

2 medium green peppers
2 medium yellow peppers
2-3 tbsps sunflower oil
1 large onion, finely sliced
2 tbsps paprika
3 medium tomatoes, skinned and quartered
2 eggs, well beaten
Cooked rice, to serve

**1.** Wash the peppers, core them and cut into strips.

**2.** Heat the oil in a large frying pan, add the onion and sauté for 1-2 minutes until just coloured.

**3.** Add the paprika, and stir well.

**4.** Add the peppers and sauté for about 2 minutes.

**5.** Add the tomatoes and cook for a further minute.

**6.** Add the beaten eggs and seasoning.

**7.** Stir well until just cooked.

**8.** Serve immediately on a bed of rice.

TIME: Preparation takes 10 minutes, cooking takes about 10 minutes.

SERVING IDEA: Lesco can be served with boiled potatoes instead of rice.

VARIATION: Red peppers may be used in place of the yellow peppers.

# NUTTY SPAGHETTI

*An easy-to-make lunch or supper dish.*

*SERVES 4*

225g/8oz spaghetti
700ml/1¼ pints boiling, salted water
2 tbsps sunflower oil
1 onion, finely chopped
2½ tsps curry powder
175ml/6 fl oz tomato juice
3 tbsps crunchy peanut butter
1 tbsp lemon juice
Lemon twists and peanuts for garnish

**1.** Boil the spaghetti in the water until 'al dente' and drain well.

**2.** Heat the oil in a frying pan, add the onion and sauté until golden brown.

**3.** Stir in the curry powder, tomato juice, peanut butter and lemon juice.

**4.** Simmer for 5 minutes and then stir into the spaghetti.

**5.** Garnish with lemon twists and peanuts.

TIME: Preparation takes about 10 minutes, cooking takes 25 minutes.

VARIATION: Almond butter and blanched almonds or tahini and sesame seeds can be used in place of the peanut butter and peanuts.

# PARSNIP FRITTERS

*These tasty fritters make a nice change for lunch or a light snack.*

*SERVES 4*

120g/4oz plain unbleached flour
2 tsps baking powder
1 tsp salt
½ tsp pepper
1 egg
140ml/¼ pint milk
1 tsp melted butter or margarine
680g/1½lbs cooked parsnips, finely diced
Oil or clarified butter for frying

**1.** Sift together the flour, baking powder, salt and pepper.

**2.** Beat the egg and mix with the milk and melted butter.

**3.** Stir this mixture into the dry ingredients.

**4.** Stir in the cooked parsnips.

**5.** Divide the mixture into 16 and shape into small fritters.

**6.** Fry in oil or clarified butter until browned on both sides.

TIME: Preparation takes 10 minutes, cooking takes about 5-8 minutes per batch.

VARIATION: Courgettes, sweetcorn, onions or aubergine may be substituted for the parsnips.

SERVING IDEA: Serve with yogurt sauce or make them slightly larger and serve as a main course with salad.

# CHICK PEAS AND BULGAR WHEAT

*High in protein and flavour, this simple lunch dish is sure to become a family favourite.*

*SERVES 4*

1 tbsp vegetable oil
2 small onions, chopped
1 red pepper, chopped
460g/1lb cooked chick peas
120g/4oz bulgar wheat
120ml/4 fl oz tomato purée
570ml/1 pint vegetable stock or water
Onion rings, to garnish

**1.** Heat the oil in a saucepan and sauté the onion and pepper until soft, but not coloured.

**2.** Stir in the chick peas and bulgar wheat. Stir in the tomato purée then gradually add the stock or water.

**3.** Bring gently to the boil, cover and simmer gently for 10-15 minutes or until the bulgar wheat is tender and the liquid has been absorbed.

**4.** Transfer to a serving dish and garnish with onion rings.

TIME: Preparation takes about 10 minutes, cooking takes about 20 minutes.

VARIATION: Use green peppers in place of the red peppers in this recipe, and add ½ tsp of chilli powder for a spicy variation.

SERVING IDEA: Serve with a crunchy carrot and peanut coleslaw.

COOK'S TIP: Care should be taken to ensure chickpeas are well cooked, they should be boiled for at least 30 minutes. As an alternative, use 460g/1lb canned chickpeas, which will require no pre-cooking.

# CHEESE AND TOMATO PASTA

*This favourite Italian classic is perfect served as a supper dish and will be popular with all the family.*

*SERVES 4*

225g/8oz tagliatelle verdi
Salt
1 tbsp vegetable oil
1 onion, chopped
120g/4oz mushrooms, finely sliced
1 tbsp tomato purée
1 × 400g/14oz can chopped tomatoes
2 tbsps dried mixed herbs
120g/4oz vegetarian Cheddar cheese, grated
Freshly ground black pepper

**1.** Cook the pasta in plenty of lightly salted boiling water for 10 minutes, until 'al dente' or as directed on the packet.

**2.** Meanwhile, heat the oil and sauté the onions until beginning to soften.

**3.** Add the mushrooms and sauté for 3 minutes. Stir in the tomato purée, tomatoes and herbs, and simmer gently whilst the pasta cooks.

**4.** When the pasta is cooked, stir most of the cheese into the tomato sauce. Season.

**5.** Drain the pasta well and pile onto a serving dish. Spoon the sauce into the centre and top with the remaining cheese.

TIME: Preparation takes about 10 minutes, cooking takes about 20 minutes.

COOK'S TIP: Fresh pasta is now readily available and very quick to cook. You will need about twice the weight of dried pasta.

SERVING IDEA: Serve with a mixed salad and hot garlic bread.

VARIATION: Use any variety of pasta shapes in this recipe.

# MUSHROOM, PEPPER AND CELERY FRITTATA

*A frittata is an Italian style omelette. If you you wish you can turn the frittata over when the vegetables are added and the bottom is thoroughly cooked.*

*SERVES 4-6*

175g/6oz mushrooms, wiped and sliced
Oil
1 medium onion, finely chopped
1-2 cloves garlic, crushed
1 small green pepper, sliced
1 small red pepper, sliced
2 sticks celery, finely chopped
5 eggs
3 tbsps water
Salt and black pepper
2-3 tbsps grated vegetarian cheddar cheese

**1.** Put the mushrooms into a small pan with a little water and cook until just softened.

**2.** Using an 18-20.5cm/7-8 inch non-stick frying pan, heat a small amount of oil and stir-fry the onion, garlic, peppers and celery for 2-3 minutes. Remove with a slotted spoon and reserve.

**3.** Beat the eggs together with the water and add the seasoning.

**4.** Return the frying pan to the heat and add a little more oil if necessary. Pour the egg mixture into the pan, allow the bottom to set a little, then sprinkle the cheese over and spoon the vegetables on top.

**5.** Lower the heat, cover and cook for 10-12 minutes until puffed and set. You may find it necessary to pull the mixture away from the sides with a pallette knife to allow the uncooked mixture to run underneath.

**6.** Loosen the edges and turn out. Cut into wedges and serve immediately.

TIME: Preparation takes 10 minutes and cooking takes about 15 minutes.

SERVING IDEA: Serve hot or cold with green beans and new potatoes.

WATCHPOINT: A good non-stick frying pan is essential for the Frittata.

# MILLET RISSOLES WITH YOGURT SAUCE

*Rissoles are always popular and yogurt sauce makes these even more tempting!*

*MAKES ABOUT 15*

1 medium onion, finely chopped
1 clove garlic, crushed
1 tsp dried mixed herbs or 2 tbsps freshly
   chopped parsley
Oil
150g/5oz millet flakes
280-420ml/½-¾ pint water
1 tbsp tomato purée
1 tsp vegetable extract
90g/3oz vegetarian Cheddar cheese, grated
¼ tsp paprika
Salt and pepper
Wholemeal breadcrumbs

**Sauce**
280ml/½ pint Greek yogurt
2 tbsps freshly chopped parsley
Salt and pepper
Pinch of paprika
A little lemon juice (optional)

**1.** Sauté the onion, garlic and mixed herbs in a little oil until soft.

**2.** Place the millet flakes in a separate pan with the water, bring to the boil and simmer gently, stirring constantly until a thick texture results.

**3.** Cool a little.

**4.** Add the remaining rissole ingredients, except the breadcrumbs, and mix together well.

**5.** Shape into rissoles and coat with the crumbs.

**6.** Fry in very shallow oil on both sides until crisp and golden.

**7.** To make the sauce, mix all the ingredients together well.

TIME: Preparation takes 15 minutes, cooking takes 15 minutes.

SERVING IDEA: Serve with the sauce handed round separately.

VARIATION: Vary the flavour of the rissoles by using freshly chopped mint instead of the mixed herbs or parsley. Fresh basil also makes a delicious alternative.

# VEGETABLE STIR FRY WITH TOFU

*The inclusion of tofu in this recipe makes it an excellent protein meal.*

*SERVES 4*

4 broccoli spears
120g/4oz baby corn
60ml/4 tbsps vegetable oil
30g/1oz blanched almonds
1 clove garlic, crushed
1 red pepper, sliced
120g/4oz mange tout, trimmed
60g/2oz water chestnuts, sliced
60ml/4 tbsps soy sauce
1 tsp sesame oil
1 tsp sherry
140ml/¼ pint vegetable stock
2 tsps cornflour
120g/4oz fresh bean sprouts
4 spring onions, cut into thin diagonal slices
225g/8oz tofu, cut into small dice
Salt and freshly ground black pepper

**1.** Remove the florets from the broccoli and set aside. Trim the broccoli stems and slice thinly.

**2.** Cut the baby corn in half lengthways.

**3.** Heat the oil in a wok or large frying pan and fry the almonds until lightly browned. Remove with a slotted spoon and set aside.

**4.** Add the garlic, broccoli stems and baby corn to the pan and stir-fry for 1 minute.

**5.** Stir in the pepper, mangetout, water chestnuts and broccoli florets and stir-fry for 3-4 minutes.

**6.** Mix the soy sauce, sesame oil, sherry, stock and cornflour together in a small dish and stir until blended.

**7.** Add to the pan and stir until sauce thickens.

**8.** Add the bean sprouts, browned almonds, spring onion and tofu and cook for 2-3 minutes.

**9.** Season to taste and serve at once.

TIME: Preparation takes about 20 minutes, cooking takes 10-12 minutes.

VARIATION: Use any combination of vegetables in season.

SERVING IDEA: Serve with boiled rice or mixed grains and seeds.

# SAVOURY RICE CAKE

*An excellent way to use up left-over rice.*

*SERVES 2*

1 medium onion, finely chopped
1 clove garlic, crushed
2 tbsps olive oil
1 tbsp fresh thyme, chopped
1 small red pepper, thinly sliced
1 small green pepper, thinly sliced
6 eggs, beaten
Salt and pepper
60g/2oz cooked brown rice
3 tbsps natural yogurt
90g/3oz Cheddar cheese, grated

**1.** Sauté the onion and garlic in the olive oil until soft.

**2.** Add the thyme and peppers and cook gently for 4-5 minutes.

**3.** Beat the eggs with the salt and pepper.

**4.** Add the cooked rice to the thyme and pepper followed by the eggs.

**5.** Cook over a moderate heat, stirring from time to time until the eggs are cooked underneath.

**6.** Spoon the yogurt on top of the part-set egg and sprinkle the cheese over the top.

**7.** Put under a moderate grill and cook until puffed and golden.

**8.** Serve immediately.

TIME: Preparation takes about 15 minutes, cooking takes 15 minutes.

SERVING IDEA: Garnish with fresh thyme and serve with a green salad and crusty bread.

# MACARONI AND BLUE CHEESE

*The classic combination of apples and blue cheese sets this delicious variation of macaroni cheese apart from its humble origins.*

*SERVES 4*

340g/12oz wholemeal macaroni
Salt
90g/3oz butter
90g/3oz plain flour
570ml/1 pint milk
1 tsp dried or fresh chopped tarragon
225g/8oz vegetarian blue cheese, crumbled
   or grated
Freshly ground black pepper
2 tbsps vegetable oil
2 apples, cored and chopped
2 onions, chopped
1 clove garlic, crushed
Sprig of fresh tarragon, to garnish

**1.** Cook the macaroni in plenty of lightly salted boiling water for 12 minutes until 'al dente' or as directed on the packet. Drain well.

**2.** Meanwhile melt the butter in a saucepan, stir in the flour, and cook for 1 minute.

**3.** Remove from the heat and gradually stir in the milk. Return to the heat and bring to the boil, stirring constantly, then simmer for 1-2 minutes.

**4.** Stir in the tarragon and blue cheese and cook until the cheese melts, taste and season with salt if needed and freshly ground pepper.

**5.** In a smaller pan heat the oil and sauté the apple, onion and garlic for 5 minutes until just soft.

**6.** Mix the apple and onion into the sauce then stir in the drained pasta, return to the heat to warm through the pasta if necessary. Serve garnished with a sprig of fresh tarragon.

TIME: Preparation takes about 5 minutes, cooking takes about 20 minutes.

VARIATION: Use sage instead of the tarragon in this recipe.

# TOFU BURGERS

*Serve these delicious burgers with mustard and pickles and accompany with a salad.*

*MAKES 8*

60g/2oz bulgar wheat
120ml/4 fl oz boiling water
1 small onion, very finely chopped
60g/2oz carrot, grated
60g/2oz mushrooms, very finely chopped
250g/9oz packet tofu
½ tsp basil
½ tsp oregano
2 tbsps shoyu sauce (Japanese soy sauce)
1 tsp tomato purée
Black pepper
Wholewheat flour
Oil for deep frying

**1.** Put the bulgar wheat into a bowl and cover with the boiling water. Leave to stand for 15 minutes until all the water has been absorbed.

**2.** Add the onion, carrot and mushrooms to the bulgar and mix well.

**3.** Drain the tofu and crumble into the bowl.

**4.** Add the basil, oregano, shoyu, tomato purée, a little black pepper and 1 tablespoon of wholewheat flour. Mix together well.

**5.** With wet hands, take heaped tablespoonful of the mixture, squeeze together well and shape into burgers.

**6.** Coat the burgers with wholewheat flour.

**7.** Heat the oil until very hot and fry the burgers 3 or 4 at a time until golden brown.

**8.** Remove and drain on kitchen paper.

TIME: Preparation takes 15 minutes, cooking takes 5 minutes per batch.

WATCHPOINT: The oil must be very hot otherwise the burgers will disintegrate.

FREEZING: It is well worth while doubling the quantity and freezing a batch of burgers. Freeze for up to 3 months. Reheat by grilling or warming in the oven.

# TRI-COLOURED TAGLIATELLE AND VEGETABLES

*A delicious Italian dish which is ideal for an informal supper party.*

*SERVES 4*

8oz/225g tri-coloured tagliatelle (mixture of tomato, spinach and egg pasta)
Salt
60g/2oz butter or vegetable margarine
1 large onion, sliced
225g/8oz broccoli florets
2 red peppers, sliced
2 cloves garlic, crushed
2 tsps chopped fresh rosemary
90g/3oz vegetarian Cheddar cheese, finely grated
Freshly ground black pepper

**1.** Cook the pasta in plenty of lightly salted boiling water for 10 minutes until 'al dente' or as directed on the packet.

**2.** Meanwhile melt half the butter or margarine in a frying pan, sauté the onion for 4 minutes, then add the broccoli and peppers and continue to cook for 5 minutes or until all the vegetables are tender.

**3.** In a separate saucepan place the garlic, rosemary and remaining butter and heat gently for a few minutes until the fat melts and the flavours combine.

**4.** When the pasta is cooked, drain well and return to the pan. Strain the garlic mixture through a sieve on to the pasta, this gives a very subtle hint of garlic and rosemary to the pasta.

**5.** Add the cooked vegetables and cheese.

**6.** Season to taste and toss well before serving.

TIME: Preparation takes about 10 minutes, cooking takes about 15 minutes.

VARIATION: Use fresh pasta and any combination of vegetables in this recipe.

# HARVEST NUTBURGERS WITH CARROT SAUCE

*The contrasting colours of the carrot and spring greens make these burgers colourful and interesting.*

*MAKES 8*

**Nutburgers**

225g/8oz mixed nuts, ground

60g/2oz porridge oats or wholemeal flour
    (or a combination of both)

1 onion, finely chopped

1 medium carrot, grated

90g/3oz cooked, chopped spring greens or
    spinach

1 dstsp chopped parsley

1 tbsp sunflower seeds

2 tbsps sunflower oil

¼ tsp caraway seeds (optional)

¼ tsp marjoram

Black pepper

1 tbsp shoyu sauce

Stock to bind

**Sauce**

225g/8oz carrots, chopped and cooked
    until tender

¼ packet silken tofu

1 tsp tomato purée

1 tsp miso

Salt and black pepper

**1.** Place all the ingredients for the nutburgers together in a large bowl in the given order. Mix together well.

**2.** Divide the mixture into 8 and shape into burgers. Place the burgers on a lightly oiled baking tray and bake in an oven preheated to 190°C/375°F/Gas Mark 5, for 10 minutes. Turn over and bake for a further 10 minutes or until the burgers are golden brown.

**3.** To make the sauce, put all the ingredients into a liquidiser or food processor and blend until smooth. Transfer to a clean saucepan, re-heat and simmer gently for 1 minute.

TIME: Preparation takes about 15 minutes and cooking takes 20 minutes.

SERVING IDEA: Serve hot with a carrot sauce, tiny new potatoes and peas.

FREEZING: The burgers freeze well for up to 3 months but be sure to freeze them individually, or separated by greaseproof paper.

# SESAME STIR-FRY

*This recipe can be prepared in advance and cooked quickly for a romantic Oriental meal for two.*

*SERVES 2*

2 tbsps vegetable oil
½ tsp grated fresh root ginger
15g/½oz sesame seeds
60g/2oz mange tout
1 stick celery, sliced'
2 baby corn, cut in half lengthways
60g/2oz water chestnuts, thinly sliced
30g/1oz mushrooms, thinly sliced
2 spring onions, sliced diagonally
½ red pepper, sliced
120g/4oz Chinese leaves, washed and
    shredded
120g/4oz bean sprouts
1 tbsp cornflour
2 tbsps soy sauce
1 tbsp sherry
½ tsp sesame oil
60ml/4 tbsps water

**1.** Heat the oil in a wok or large frying pan and stir-fry the ginger and sesame seeds for 1 minute.

**2.** Add the mange tout, celery, baby corn, water chestnuts, mushrooms, onions and pepper, and stir-fry for 3-4 minutes or until the vegetables are tender-crisp.

**3.** Add the Chinese leaves and bean sprouts and toss over the heat for 1-2 minutes.

**4.** Combine the remaining ingredients in a small bowl, and add to the pan.

**5.** Continue cooking until sauce thickens slightly and serve immediately.

TIME: Preparation takes about 15 minutes, cooking takes about 10 minutes.

VARIATION: Use any combination of vegetables according to what you have at hand.

# PASTA SPIRALS WITH WALNUTS AND STILTON

*The classic combination of walnuts and Stilton in this recipe creates an unusual but delicious Italian style meal.*

*SERVES 4*

460g/1lb pasta spirals
Salt
280ml/½ pint double cream
460g/1lb vegetarian Stilton cheese
120g/4oz walnut halves
Freshly ground black pepper
4 sprigs fresh thyme, to garnish
2 ripe figs, to garnish

**1.** Cook the pasta in plenty of lightly salted boiling water for 10 minutes, until 'al dente' or as directed on the packet.

**2.** Place the cream in a saucepan and bring to the boil. Boil rapidly for 3 minutes, then reduce the heat, crumble in the Stilton cheese and stir until cheese melts.

**3.** Stir in the walnut halves and season with pepper.

**4.** When the pasta is cooked, drain well and return to the pan.

**5.** Pour the cream and cheese sauce onto the pasta and toss well.

**6.** Serve garnished with sprigs of thyme and half a ripe fig.

TIME: Preparation takes about 5 minutes, cooking takes about 20 minutes.

VARIATION: Use hazelnuts and vegetarian Cheshire cheese or peanuts and vegetarian Cheddar cheese, for two interesting variations.

COOK'S TIP: The walnut sauce or either of the variations, make a superb fondue sauce into which can be dipped crusty bread or fresh vegetables.

# FRUIT-FILLED MELON

*A refreshing, easy-to-prepare dessert that relies on a colourful combination of different fruits for its effect.*

*SERVES 4*

2 melons
1 orange, peeled
2 figs, cut into slices
1 green apple, thinly sliced
1 red apple, thinly sliced
1 kiwi, cut into round slices
1 bunch grapes
12 raspberries
Sugar

**1.** Cut the melons in half using a sharp knife. If necessary, cut a thin slice off the bottom of the melon halves so that they are stable.

**2.** Scrape out the seeds with a small spoon and discard. Using a melon-baller, cut five or six small balls from the centre of each melon half.

**3.** Cut the orange into segments and remove the skin. Wash, halve and deseed the grapes.

**4.** Put all the fruit, including the melon balls, in to the melon halves. Chill until ready to serve. A little sugar can be sprinkled over the fruit, if required.

TIME: Preparation takes about 20 minutes.

VARIATION: Use different fruit to fill the melons, according to season.

COOK'S TIP: A spoonful of port makes a delicious addition to the fruit.

# HOT FRUIT SALAD CUPS

*These attractive cups of warm fresh fruit make a delightful and slightly more unusual ending to a meal.*

*SERVES 4*

2 large oranges
1 small dessert apple
1 slice fresh pineapple
1 banana
A little orange juice
30g/1oz caster sugar
1 tsp rum
15g/½oz pistachio nuts, skin removed,
  chopped
Orange zest, to decorate (optional)

**1.** Cut the oranges in half and using a grapefruit knife, remove the flesh and membranes, leaving just the white pith and zest to form a shell; set aside. Reserve as much juice as possible and chop the flesh discarding the membranes.

**2.** Cut the apples into quarters, remove the core, but do not peel. Cut each quarter into bite-size pieces.

**3.** Remove the skin and the tough core from the pineapple and cut into bite-size pieces. Peel and slice the banana.

**4.** Make the reserved juice up to 140ml/¼ pint with extra orange juice, if necessary. Heat the juice and sugar and stir until dissolved. Stir in the rum.

**5.** Mix the prepared fruit into the juice. Just before serving, heat gently to warm the fruit, but not cook it.

**6.** Pile into orange shells and sprinkle with chopped pistachio nuts. Decorate with orange zest if wished and serve immediately.

TIME: Preparation takes about 15 minutes, cooking time is about 5 minutes.

VARIATION: Use any combination of your favourite fruit to fill the orange shells in this recipe.

# SAUTÉED APPLES WITH CALVADOS

*This dessert uses two of the Normandy region's most famous products to create a true taste of France.*

*SERVES 4*

4 small apples
30g/1oz butter
2 tbsps sugar
30g/1oz flaked almonds
2 tbsps raisins
2 tbsps Calvados

**1.** Peel and core the apples and cut them into even-sized pieces.

**2.** Heat the butter and add the apples. Sauté until lightly coloured then add the sugar.

**3.** Add the almonds and raisins and sauté for a further 2 minutes.

**4.** Flame the mixture with the Calvados, sauté for a further minute and serve immediately.

TIME: Preparation takes about 15 minutes and cooking about 10 minutes.

SERVING IDEA: A custard sauce flavoured with cinnamon would go particularly well with this dish.

VARIATION: Try different liqueurs such as rum, Armagnac etc.

WATCHPOINT: Take care when you flame the sautéed apples as the flame can go quite high.

# BAKED BANANAS SAUCE A LA POIRE

*Baked bananas are an established favourite for dessert and served with this delightful fruity sauce they are particularly delicious.*

*SERVES 4*

2 small oranges
2 ripe pears, peeled and cored
Honey, to taste
4 bananas

**1.** Using a swivel vegetable peeler pare the rind from one of the oranges, taking care not to include too much white pith.

**2.** Cut the pared rind into very thin strips with a sharp knife and blanch in boiling water for 2-3 minutes, to soften. Drain and set aside.

**3.** Cut off all the remaining pith from the orange using a sharp knife and slice the segments out from the membrane. Squeeze the juice from the other orange.

**4.** Place the orange juice and pears into a food processor and purée until smooth. Sweeten to taste with honey.

**5.** Peel the bananas, place in an oven-proof dish and pour the pear purée over the top. Cover and bake in an oven preheated to 180°C/350°F/Gas Mark 4, for 15 minutes or until the bananas are soft.

**6.** Decorate with the orange segments and strips of orange rind and serve immediately.

TIME: Preparation takes about 10 minutes, cooking time is about 15 minutes.

VARIATION: Use pineapple instead of pears in this recipe, and sprinkle 1 tbsp flaked coconut over the finished dish.

PREPARATION: This dessert is best prepared as late as possible to prevent discolouration of the fruit.

SERVING IDEA: Serve with biscuits and some cream.

# Index